W9-BWK-656

3 5674 03607559 7

Title Withdrawn

Edison Branch Library
18400 Joy Rd.
Detroit, MI 48228
(313) 852-4515

JR-ED

NOV 03 Cont.

Issue #2
Fall 2003

biography
for
beginners

Sketches for Early Readers

Laurie Lanzen Harris,
Editor

Favorable Impressions

P.O. Box 69018
Pleasant Ridge, Michigan 48069

Laurie Lanzen Harris, *Editor and Publisher*
Dan Harris, *Vice President, Marketing*
Favorable Impressions
P.O. Box 69018, Pleasant Ridge, Michigan 48069

Copyright © 2003 Laurie Lanzen Harris

ISSN 1081-4973

All rights reserved. No part of this publication may be reproduced or transmit-
ted in any form or by any means, electronic or mechanical, including photocopy,
recording, or any information storage and retrieval system, without permission
in writing from the publisher.

The information in this publication was compiled from the sources cited and
from other sources considered reliable. While every possible effort has been
made to ensure reliability, the publisher will not assume liability for damages
caused by inaccuracies in the data, and makes no warranty, express or im-
plied, on the accuracy of the information contained herein.

(∞)

This book is printed on acid-free paper meeting the ANSI Z39.48 Standard. The
infinity symbol that appears above indicates that the paper in this book meets
that standard.

Printed in the United States

Contents

Preface

Biography for Beginners is a publication designed for young readers ages 6 to 9. It covers the kinds of people young people want to know about—favorite authors, television and sports stars, and world figures.

Biography for Beginners is published two times a year. A one-year subscription includes two 100-page hardbound volumes, published in Spring (May) and Fall (October).

The Plan of the Work

Biography for Beginners is especially created for young readers in a format they can read, understand, and enjoy. Each hardcover issue contains approximately 10 profiles, arranged alphabetically. Each entry provides several illustrations, including photographs of the individual, book covers, illustrations from books, and action shots. Each entry is coded with a symbol that indicates the profession of the person profiled. Boldfaced headings lead readers to information on birth, growing up, school, choosing a career, work life, and home and family. Each entry concludes with an address so that students can write for further information. Web sites are included as available. The length and vocabulary used in each entry, as well as the type size, page size, illustrations, and layout, have been developed with early readers in mind.

Because an early reader's first introduction to biography often comes as part of a unit on a writer like Dr. Seuss, authors are a special focus of *Biography for Beginners*. The authors included in this issue were chosen for their appeal to readers in grades one through four.

There is a broad range of reading abilities in children ages 6 to 9. A book that would appeal to a beginning first-grade reader might not satisfy the needs of an advanced reader finishing the fourth grade. To accommodate the widest range of readers in the age group, *Biography for Beginners* is written at the mid-second grade to third grade reading level. If beginning readers find the content too difficult, the entry could be used as a "read aloud" text, or readers could use the boldfaced headings to focus on parts of a sketch.

Indexes

Each issue of *Biography for Beginners* includes a Name Index, a Subject Index covering occupations and ethnic and minority backgrounds, and a Birthday Index. These indexes cumulate with each issue. The indexes are intended to be used by the young readers themselves, with help from teachers and librarians, and are not as detailed or lengthy as the indexes in works for older children.

Our Advisors

Biography for Beginners was reviewed by an Advisory Board made up of school librarians, public librarians, and reading specialists. Their thoughtful comments and suggestions have been invaluable in developing this publication. Any errors, however, are mine alone. I would like to list the members of the Advisory Board and to thank them again for their efforts.

Gail Beaver   University of Michigan School of Information
Ann Arbor, MI

Nancy Bryant   Brookside School Library
Cranbrook Educational Community
Bloomfield Hills, MI

Linda Carpino   Detroit Public Library
Detroit, MI

Helen Gregory   Grosse Pointe Public Library
Grosse Pointe, MI

Your Comments Are Welcome

Our goal is to provide accurate, accessible biographical information to early readers. Let us know how you think we're doing. Please write or call me with your comments.

We want to include the people your young readers want to know about. Send me your suggestions to the address below, or to my e-mail address. You can also post suggestions at our website, www.favimp.com. If we include someone you or a young reader suggest, we will send you a free issue, with our compliments, and we'll list your name in the issue in which your suggested profile appears.

And take a look at the next page, where we've listed those libraries and individuals who will be receiving a free copy of this issue for their suggestions.

Acknowledgments

I'd like to thank Mary Ann Stavros for superb design, layout, and typesetting; Cherie Abbey for editorial assistance; Barry Puckett for research assistance; and Kevin Hayes for production help.

Laurie Harris
Editor, *Biography for Beginners*
P.O. Box 69018
Pleasant Ridge, MI 48069
e-mail: Llanzenh@aol.com
URL: http://www.favimp.com

CONGRATULATIONS!

Congratulations to the following individuals and libraries, who are receiving a free copy of *Biography for Beginners*, Fall 2003, for suggesting people who appear in this issue:

Sister Jeanette Adler, Pine Ridge Elementary School, Birdseye, IN
Lydia Carswell, Palmer River Elementary School, Rehoboth, MA
D. Kirby, Custer Elementary School, Lakewood, WA
Marcy McAdoo, Judith Resnik Elementary School, Gaithersburg, MD
Deborah Rothaug, Pasadena Elementary School, Plainview, NY

Ben Carson
1951-
American Neurosurgeon and Author

BEN CARSON WAS BORN on September 18, 1951, in Detroit, Michigan. His full name is Benjamin Solomon Carson. His parents were Robert and Sonya Carson. He has one older brother, Curtis.

BEN CARSON GREW UP in Detroit in a poor family and a rough neighborhood. His parents divorced when Ben was eight. Ben and Curtis lived with their mom. Sonya Carson worked long hours cleaning houses to support her family. Money was tight. Carson remembers that "whenever Curtis or I asked for toys or candy, we heard the same answer: 'we just don't have the money'."

BEN CARSON WENT TO SCHOOL at Higgins Elementary in Detroit. He didn't like school, and he didn't do well, either. He thought he was the "dumbest kid in school." Kids teased him, and he faced racism, too. White kids threatened him at school, on the playground, and even walking home. It made him sad, and angry, too.

Then his mom stepped in and made some changes. Sonya Carson had only gone to school through the third grade, but she knew the importance of education. She thought Ben and Curtis weren't doing well in school because they watched too much TV. So she limited them to three hours a week.

Instead, the boys had to read two books a week. They also had to write a book report on each book. The boys complained, but the extra reading made a difference. Ben went from the bottom to the top of his class.

At Wilson Junior High, Carson won an award as the highest-achieving student. But he still faced racism. At the awards assembly, a teacher "bawled out the white kids because they had allowed me to be number one," Carson recalled.

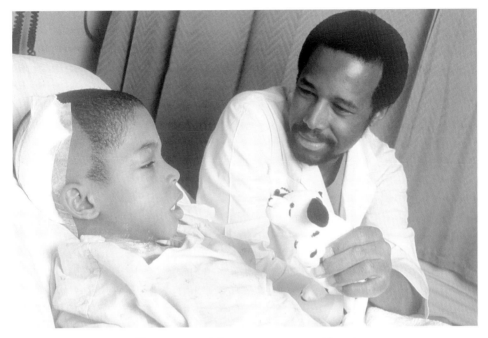

Carson with a young patient.

Despite his success in school, Carson was often angry and unhappy. As a teenager, he sometimes let his hot temper get the best of him. He fought with his brother and with friends. Once, he tried to stab a friend in anger. Luckily for everyone, the knife broke against the friend's belt. The friend was unharmed, and Ben had a chance to change.

The incident really turned Carson around. He shut himself in the bathroom and read the Bible. "It said that mightier is the person who can control his temper than the one who can run the city," he recalled. "I realized I was my own worst enemy and that a weak person is controlled by anger."

Edison Branch Library
18400 Joy Rd.
Detroit, MI 48228
(313) 852-4515

11

Guided by his religious faith and his mother's love, Carson set out to be the best person he could be. He was an outstanding student at Southwestern High School. He played in the band and worked in the lab after school. He did so well that he won a scholarship to Yale University, one of the best colleges in the country.

DECIDING TO BECOME A DOCTOR: Carson studied hard at Yale. College was tough, but he was determined to do well. He majored in psychology and decided he wanted to be a doctor. After graduating in 1973, he went to medical school at the University of Michigan. When he started med school, Carson planned to become a psychiatrist. (A psychiatrist has a medical degree and specializes in human psychology.) As part of his medical training, he studied surgery. He loved it. Carson decided to become a neurosurgeon.

BECOMING A NEUROSURGEON: "Neurology" is the study of the brain, spinal cord, and nerves. A neurosurgeon specializes in operations on this incredibly important — and delicate — area of the body. Neurosurgeons deal with life-threatening conditions — like a tumor growing in the brain or an injury to the spinal cord.

After finishing medical school in 1977, Carson continued his training at Johns Hopkins in Baltimore, Maryland. That is one of the finest medical facilities in the world.

During his training, he spent a year at a hospital in Australia. There, he performed several brain surgeries. He removed tumors from patients' brains that allowed them to lead normal lives.

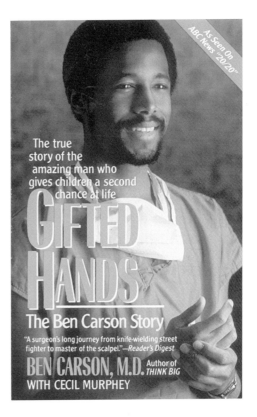

The true story of the amazing man who gives children a second chance at life

GIFTED HANDS

The Ben Carson Story

"A surgeon's long journey from knife-wielding street fighter to master of the scalpel."—*Reader's Digest*

BEN CARSON, M.D. Author of *THINK BIG*
WITH CECIL MURPHEY

CHIEF OF PEDIATRIC NEUROSURGERY:
Returning to Johns Hopkins in 1984, Carson was named chief of "pediatric neurosurgery." That is a neurosurgeon who specializes in children's needs. His patients had many serious medical problems. Some had brain tumors, and some suffered from seizures and other serious conditions.

The brain controls almost all movement and behavior. Scientists are still discovering exactly how each part of the brain works, but they do know what happens when things go wrong. A tumor can press on areas of the brain that control speech and movement. Seizures can cause brain damage and death.

In one case, Carson performed surgery on a four-year-old girl who was having over 100 seizures a day. He removed a portion of her brain. The little girl recovered completely, and now lives a normal life.

A FAMOUS OPERATION: One of Carson's most serious cases involved a pair of twins, Patrick and Benjamin. They were "conjoined" twins, who were born with the back of their heads grown together. Conjoined twins are separate infants who share some body parts. (Twins born connected in this way are sometimes called Siamese twins.) Surgery to separate them is very difficult and risky.

Carson's job was to try to separate the twins, including the brain and surrounding blood vessels. The surgery had never been performed successfully. There was a large risk that both babies might die, or suffer brain damage.

The operation took place on September 5, 1987. Carson headed a team of 70 doctors and nurses. It took 22 hours to separate the boys, but Carson and his team did it.

The success of the operation made Carson famous. He became known around the world for his skill. And as people learned of his achievement in medicine, they also learned of his life story. Many were moved by his journey to success.

"I came to understand that the life I've had is unusual," remembers Carson. "Many people who have yet to achieve could probably identify with it. My biggest

Carson speaks to a group of young students.

mission was to see if perhaps something could be done, using the example of my life, to encourage others to develop a 'can do' as opposed to a 'what-can-you-do-for-me' attitude."

To share his story, Carson wrote several books about his remarkable life. In books like *Gifted Hands, THINK BIG,* and *The Big Picture,* he tells how he achieved his dreams. But most importantly, he encourages people, especially young people, to make their own dreams come true.

"Think big," says Carson, referring to his book. "Each letter in the two words represents something: **T**alent,

Honesty, Insight, Nice, Knowledge; Books, In-depth learning, and God. I guarantee that anyone who follows those tips will succeed."

Carson continues to perform 500 to 600 surgeries every year. He still loves his work. His favorite part is telling the worried parents of a patient: "Your child is awake and asking for you." "To me, that is a highlight," says Carson. "I love it."

BEN CARSON'S HOME AND FAMILY: Carson met his wife, Candy, while he was in college. She is a musician. They have three sons, Murray, Ben Jr., and Rhoeyce. The family lives in a home near Baltimore with three generations of Carsons: Ben and Candy, their sons, and Ben's mom, Sonya.

Carson visits schools and youth groups often. He tells children about his own life. He wants them to know that they can achieve whatever they want, if they're willing to work hard. He and his wife started a scholarship program, the Carson Scholars Fund. It provides money for college scholarships for kids.

Carson is a very religious man. He believes that faith has guided his life and his success. "God's hand is still at work in my life," he says. "Do your best, and let God do the rest."

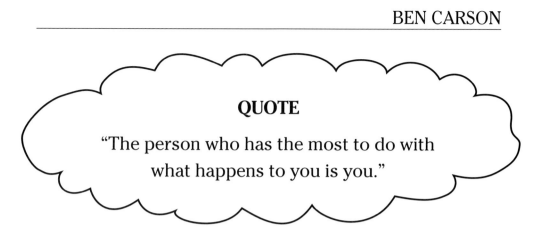

QUOTE

"The person who has the most to do with
what happens to you is you."

FOR MORE INFORMATION ABOUT BEN CARSON:

Write: Johns Hopkins Medical Institutions
Meyer 5-109
600 N. Wolfe
Baltimore, MD 21205

WORLD WIDE WEB SITES:

http://www.drbencarson.com
http://www.topblacks.com/medicine/ben-carson.htm
http://www.carolina.com/carson/index.asp

Dick Cheney
1941-
American Vice President

DICK CHENEY WAS BORN on January 30, 1941, in
Lincoln, Nebraska. His full name is Richard Bruce Cheney.
His last name is pronounced CHAY-nee. His parents were
Marjorie and Richard H. Cheney. His mother was a home-
maker and his father worked for the Department of
Agriculture. He has a brother, Bob, and a sister, Susan.

DICK CHENEY GREW UP first in Nebraska and then in Wyoming. His family moved to Casper, Wyoming, when he was 13. He loved the state, and he still has a home there.

DICK CHENEY WENT TO SCHOOL at College View Elementary in Lincoln, Nebraska. After moving to Wyoming, he went to Natrona County High. He was an excellent student and especially loved history. Cheney was captain of the football team and president of his senior class.

His football coach, Harry Geldien, remembers Cheney's quiet leadership. "The team would be dressing for a game, and there was usually a lot of chattering and noise. But when Dick started to speak, the other kids would stop and listen. They respected him."

Dick also met the woman who would become his wife, Lynne Vincent. She was an excellent student and a champion baton-twirler. They dated throughout high school.

One of the local businessmen took an interest in Cheney's education. He encouraged Cheney to apply to Yale University. Cheney attended Yale on a full scholarship. But he didn't do well, and he missed Wyoming. So he left after three semesters and moved home.

Cheney spent the next few years working as a lineman for a local electric company. Then he decided to

Cheney (center) with his high school football team.

return to college. He attended the University of Wyoming and studied political science. (That's the study of government and politics.) He had stayed in touch with Lynne, who was attending Colorado College. They married in 1964. Cheney received his bachelor's degree in 1965 and his master's degree in 1966.

Cheney loved political science. He decided he wanted to continue his education and teach college. In 1967, the Cheney family moved to Wisconsin. He'd been accepted at the University of Wisconsin to study for a doctoral degree (Ph.D.).

GETTING INVOLVED IN POLITICS: But Dick Cheney never finished his Ph.D. He got an offer to work for Wisconsin Congressman Bill Steiger. So the family moved to Washington, D.C., in 1968.

In 1969, Cheney took his first job working for the federal government. The job was in the Office of Economic Opportunity. His boss was Donald Rumsfeld. The two would work together often over the next 35 years.

WORKING FOR GERALD FORD: In 1974, Cheney took a job in the White House working for President Gerald Ford. He became Ford's Chief of Staff in 1975. In that job, he coordinated the work of the President's White House staff. He was just 34, the youngest person ever to hold the job. Ford ran for President in 1976, but lost to Jimmy Carter. Cheney returned to Wyoming.

A U.S. REPRESENTATIVE: Back in Wyoming, Cheney decided to run for the U.S. House of Representatives. In 1978, he ran as a Republican and won Wyoming's only seat in the House. Cheney was a very popular representative and was re-elected five times. He chaired several important committees and became a Republican party leader. He was named the Republican "whip." That is what the assistant leader of the House of Representatives is called.

SECRETARY OF DEFENSE: In 1989, President George Bush asked Cheney to be the Secretary of Defense. The Secretary of Defense is a member of the President's Cabinet of advisors. The Secretary is head of the U.S. armed forces and advises the President on all military issues.

As Secretary of Defense, Cheney advised President Bush during the Persian Gulf War. The war was fought in the Persian Gulf region of the Middle East in 1990-1991. In August 1990, Iraq, led by Saddam Hussein, invaded Kuwait. President Bush and other world leaders demanded that Iraq withdraw its troops. Iraq refused. Cheney helped to put together troops from the U.S. and other countries from the United Nations. Together, they challenged Hussein. The allied forces, called "Desert Storm," attacked the Iraqis on land and in bombing raids. The Gulf War lasted only 100 hours. The Iraqis were beaten and withdrew from Kuwait.

The war was a great success for the U.S. and its allies. For his leadership in the Gulf War, Cheney received the Presidential Medal of Freedom. He continued as Secretary of Defense until 1992, when Bush lost his re-election race to Bill Clinton. Cheney moved back to the West.

A BUSINESSMAN: In 1995, Cheney became chairman and CEO (Chief Executive Officer) of the Halliburton

President Gerald R. Ford with Cheney, November 7, 1975, when he was Ford's Chief of Staff.

Company. Halliburton is a Texas construction and engineering company. He worked in that job for five years.

In 2000, Cheney got a call from George W. Bush. Bush, the son of his former boss, was running for President. He asked Cheney to help him find a good Vice Presidential running mate. Cheney worked for

Cheney with Colin Powell during the Gulf War, December 21, 1990, when Cheney was Secretary of Defense.

several months, interviewing candidates. Then, to his surprise, Bush chose him to be his running mate.

VICE PRESIDENT OF THE UNITED STATES: Bush and Cheney won the election of 2000, and Dick Cheney became the Vice President of the United States.

It is the Vice President's role to take over if the President becomes ill or dies. He is also the leader of the Senate and can cast tie-breaking votes on bills.

But Cheney's most important job is to help President Bush achieve his goals for the country. Cheney has a great deal of knowledge about how the government works. He knows about Congress, and he knows about international politics and the military.

All of that background makes Cheney a very effective Vice President. President Bush is able to rely on his advice and knowledge in dealing with the country's problems. After the terrorist attacks of September 11, 2001, Cheney worked closely with the President and his team of advisors. Together, they developed a plan to make the country safe and to fight terrorism. In 2003, the U.S. was once again fighting against Saddam Hussein in Iraq. Cheney's experience has helped the President in determining U.S. policy there and around the world.

HEALTH CONCERNS: This hard-working man has had his share of medical problems. He has heart disease and has had several heart attacks. To fight the disease, he's had surgery and made changes in his lifestyle. He's careful to eat properly and get enough exercise.

Soon after the 2000 election, Cheney had more problems with his heart. In 2001 he had a pacemaker implanted in his chest. It helps his heart to beat normally. Cheney and his doctors are confident that he is doing well now. He plans to serve his country for years to come.

Vice President Cheney with President Bush, January 2003.

RUNNING FOR RE-ELECTION: In May 2003, Cheney announced that President Bush had asked him to run with him again in the election of 2004. He accepted and is looking forward to being Bush's running mate again.

DICK CHENEY'S HOME AND FAMILY: Cheney married his high school sweetheart, Lynne, in 1964. They have two daughters, Elizabeth and Mary, and three granddaughters. In his spare time, Vice President Cheney enjoys reading and fishing. He also enjoys playing with his dogs, Jackson and Dave. His favorite book for kids is *The Cat in the Hat*.

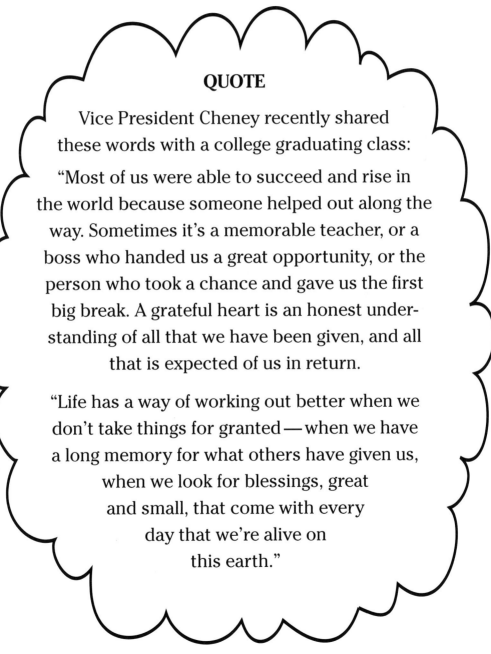

QUOTE

Vice President Cheney recently shared these words with a college graduating class:

"Most of us were able to succeed and rise in the world because someone helped out along the way. Sometimes it's a memorable teacher, or a boss who handed us a great opportunity, or the person who took a chance and gave us the first big break. A grateful heart is an honest understanding of all that we have been given, and all that is expected of us in return.

"Life has a way of working out better when we don't take things for granted—when we have a long memory for what others have given us, when we look for blessings, great and small, that come with every day that we're alive on this earth."

FOR MORE INFORMATION ABOUT DICK CHENEY:

Write: The Office of the Vice President
The White House
1600 Pennsylvania Ave.
Washington, DC 20500

WORLD WIDE WEB SITE:

http://www.whitehouse.gov/kids

Linda Ellerbee

1944-
American TV Journalist
Host of "Nick News"

LINDA ELLERBEE WAS BORN on August 15, 1944, in
Bryan, Texas. Her name when she was born was Linda
Jane Smith. Her parents were Hallie and Lonnie Ray
Smith. Hallie was a homemaker and Lonnie worked for an
insurance company. Linda was an only child.

LINDA ELLERBEE GREW UP in Bryan, then in Houston. Her parents moved to Houston when she was four. Linda also spent a great deal of time in Trinity, Texas. That is a small town out in the country where her parents had grown up.

Linda loved spending time in Trinity. She had a large family of uncles, aunts, and cousins. She rode her bike, climbed trees, visited neighbors, and played with friends.

READING: The curious and energetic young girl also spent a lot of time reading. She loved everything from comic books to novels. "It never occurred to me that I would be a journalist. But I always knew I loved to read. Books took me inside myself first. Then they took me everywhere else. I am a writer now because I was a reader then."

She says that *Little Women* by Louisa May Alcott was her favorite book. She loved the character Jo. Jo was a girl "who wrote, who was a storyteller, who had opinions, who wasn't afraid to express them."

WRITING: Linda loved to write as a child, too. "I became a journalist because of my grandmother," she claims. "She gave me my first diary for my 10th birthday." In it, she wrote down her secret thoughts. "My mother had this feeling that I deserved no privacy," says Ellerbee. "There was no closet, no drawer that she wouldn't go through." But Linda's diary was safe. "I began to write in that diary to secure something private and away from my mom."

FIRST THOUGHTS ON TELEVISION: Ellerbee also remembers hating television as a child. She was young when TV sets first appeared in American homes. She was shocked to see how many people gave up their activities to watch TV. She remembers that when she was eight, "a television ate my best friend."

"Maybe the TV hadn't actually eaten her. But she may as well have been dead. Once they pointed her in the direction of that box, she never looked up and never looked back."

TV had the same effect on her parents. Soon they were eating dinner in front of the set. "During dinner, we used to talk to one another. Now television talked to us." She never forgot how lonely that made her feel.

LINDA ELLERBEE WENT TO SCHOOL at the local public schools in Houston. She felt lonely there, too. "I just didn't fit into any particular group, and I think I wanted to," she recalls. "I was a shy kid, but not a quiet one. I used my mouth as a weapon, which often backfired."

In high school, she became interested in art and writing. She considered a career as an artist, but decided

Ellerbee on "Nick News."

to concentrate on writing. She graduated from high school in 1962 and went on to college at Vanderbilt University in Nashville, Tennessee. She dropped out of college after two years to get married.

FIRST JOBS: Ellerbee and her first husband, Mac Smith, moved to Chicago. While he was in school, she worked for a magazine and a radio station. After that marriage ended in 1966, she moved back to Houston. There, she worked for a radio station and met her second husband, Van Veselka. They lived in Texas, then moved to Alaska. She had two children, Vanessa and Joshua, before she and Veselka divorced.

GETTING INTO JOURNALISM: Ellerbee moved back to Houston in 1972 and got a job with the Associated Press (AP). AP is a news service that provides stories for news organizations around the world. She wrote for AP for six months, then got a job reporting for a Houston TV station.

Ellerbee worked for KHOU, the CBS station in Houston, for several months. In 1973, she moved to New York City to work for the CBS station there. After two years, she got a job with NBC News.

NBC NEWS: Ellerbee worked for NBC News for 12 years. Her first job was as a reporter covering national politics from Washington, D.C. After three years in that job, she became co-anchor of "Weekend," a weekly news magazine. Ellerbee became known as a reporter who covered the news with intelligence, wit, and warmth.

After "Weekend" was cancelled in 1979, Ellerbee worked for "NBC Nightly News" for three years. In 1982, she became the co-anchor of "NBC News Overnight." The show ran from 1:30 a.m. to 2:30 a.m. Despite the late hour, "Overnight" had many dedicated fans. It won several awards, including the Columbia duPont Award. That's one of the most important honors in broadcasting. They called the show "possibly the best written and most intelligent news program ever."

But NBC cancelled "Overnight" in 1983. Ellerbee continued to work for NBC until 1986, when she left to work for ABC. During two years at ABC, she wrote and anchored shows for "Our World," a documentary series. When that show was cancelled in 1987, she decided to quit.

LUCKY DUCK: Ellerbee was ready for a new challenge. So she and her partner, Rolfe Tessem, started Lucky Duck Productions.

The company is named for Ellerbee's good-luck charm, a stuffed duck. She keeps it on the set wherever she works. Over the years she and Tessem have created and produced TV shows for many networks. Their shows have appeared on major networks, like NBC and ABC, as well as PBS and cable stations. But their best-known show is "Nick News."

"NICK NEWS": It all started in 1991. That year, the U.S. led a U.N. coalition in a war against Iraq. That conflict, called the Gulf War, was the major news story for months. The president of Nickelodeon called Ellerbee and asked if she would produce a show on the war for kids. Ellerbee did, and it was a huge success. It became the first show of what would become "Nick News."

"Nick News" is the only weekly news show written and produced for kids. In addition to the weekly show, Ellerbee has also done specials on news stories of particular interest.

Ellerbee on "Nick News."

Over the years, she has covered many tough topics honestly and sensitively. Some of these shows have dealt with typical news issues, like the wars in Iraq or the Balkans. Some have dealt with national political issues, like the scandal involving Bill Clinton and Monica Lewinsky. And Ellerbee has presented shows on topics like the September 11 terrorist attacks and the Oklahoma City bombings. It is important, she says, to talk about the fear these horrible events inspired. In her programs, Ellerbee tries to offer information, and comfort, to her viewers.

Sometimes "Nick News"deals with more personal issues. These shows discuss bullying, racism, AIDS, or what life is like for the disabled.

Ellerbee is known for her straightforward yet sensitive approach. She sits among a group of kids, usually ages 8 to 14, who discuss the topic. She acts as a moderator for questions and answers. She really listens to the kids.

Most recently, Ellerbee presented a show on the current Iraq war. She had kids from a variety of backgrounds. Some came from Islamic homes. Some had moms and dads in the army. Some had protested the war. "You let the children vent and try to reassure them that the adults are working to keep them safe," she says.

As her many viewers know, Ellerbee treats her young audience with respect. "We started from the notion that we would never talk down to our audience. These kids are smart," she says.

GET REAL: In 2000, Ellerbee started a series of books for young readers. Called *Get Real*, the books feature the feisty Casey Smith. Casey is an 11-year-old girl reporter. She's based on Ellerbee's own childhood and the stories she's heard from kids. Remembering her own life, Ellerbee notes she "wasn't perfect. So when I wrote *Get Real* I wanted to write about kids who were great — kids who lived in and were passionate about a very real world — but kids who weren't perfect."

"Writing for kids is truly special. With kids, it's not about asking why. It's also about what ought to be. It's about hope. And it just doesn't get any better than that."

LINDA ELLERBEE'S HOME AND FAMILY: Ellerbee has been married and divorced four times. Her first husband was named Mac Smith. They were married from 1964 to 1966. With her second husband, Van Veselka, she had two children, Vanessa and Joshua. That marriage lasted from 1968 to 1971. In 1973, she married Tom Ellerbee. They divorced in 1974, but Ellerbee continues to use his last name. From 1976 to 1978 she was married to John David Klein. In the 1980s, she began Lucky Duck with Rolfe Tessem, who is also her boyfriend.

Ellerbee has faced some serious medical problems. In 1992, she learned she had breast cancer. She had surgery and chemotherapy. She's healthy now, and says that the experience taught her a lot. "If this is the worst thing that happens to me in my life, I will be *so* grateful. I do work that I love, I'm in a relationship with a wonderful man, my kids are healthy, and we get along."

Ellerbee lives in New York, just a few blocks from the Lucky Duck studio.

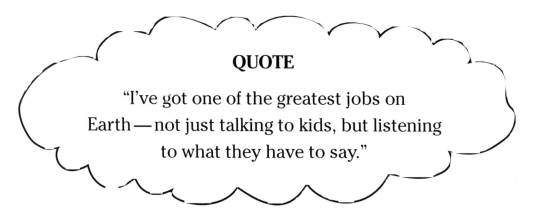

QUOTE

"I've got one of the greatest jobs on Earth—not just talking to kids, but listening to what they have to say."

SOME BOOKS BY LINDA ELLERBEE:

Get Real Series

Girl Reporter Blows Lid Off Town!
Girl Reporter Sinks School!
Girl Reporter Stuck in a Jam!
Girl Reporter Snags Crush!
Ghoul Reporter Digs Up Zombies!
Girl Reporter Rocks Polls!
Girl Reporter Gets the Skinny!
Girl Reporter Bytes Back!

FOR MORE INFORMATION ON LINDA ELLERBEE:

Write: Lucky Duck Productions
96 Morton Street
6th Floor
New York, NY 10014

WORLD WIDE WEB SITE:

http://www.nick.com/all_nick/tv_shows/

Ian Falconer
1959-
American Author, Illustrator, and Set Designer
Creator of *Olivia*

IAN FALCONER WAS BORN in 1959 in Ridgefield, Connecticut. He does not reveal a lot of information about his early years. He has a sister named Victoria.

IAN FALCONER GREW UP in Connecticut. He was a shy boy. "Although I had a very active imagination, I was very shy in front of other people," he recalls. But he did share something with his famous character, Olivia. "I dressed up a lot," he says.

Ian had a dog named Runzel and a seagull named Henry. Henry had been abandoned by his original owners. After several years with Ian's family, Henry was released back into the wild.

Ian loved to read and had several favorite books. Among them are *The 500 Hats of Bartholomew Cubbins*, *Higglety Pigglety Pop!* and *Eloise*.

IAN FALCONER WENT TO SCHOOL at the Long Ridge School in Stamford, Connecticut. For high school, he went to the Cambridge School of Weston in Massachusetts. Both schools allowed him to explore his artistic talents.

Falconer attended New York University for college. He studied art and art history. After two years there, he transferred to Parson's School of Design, also in New York. There, he studied painting. Falconer decided to move to California. He continued to study painting at the Otis Art Institute in Los Angeles.

STARTING TO WORK AS AN ARTIST: After college, Falconer began to make his living as an artist. He worked with a famous artist named David Hockney. With Hockney, Falconer designed sets and costumes for opera. He also began to create set designs for ballets.

Over the years, Falconer has worked with some of the finest opera and ballet companies in the world. He's created costumes and sets for the Chicago Lyric Opera and the Royal Opera in London. He's created sets for the

New York City Ballet and their ballet school. He's also become an illustrator for magazines like *The New Yorker.* He even designed floats for Disneyland.

HOW OLIVIA CAME TO BE: Falconer moved from L.A. to New York in the mid-1990s. He worked as an artist, and also spent time with his sister Victoria and her family. When Victoria's daughter, Olivia, was three, her Uncle Ian started working on a special present.

"I thought I'd do a little book for her, a little story," he says. And it just got better and better. "I just did the drawings first — I drew the whole story — and then I wrote it."

The book he'd created for Olivia featured a feisty little pig named for her. Falconer kept working at it. He took it to an agency. They loved the drawings. But Falconer was not a published author. So they offered to use the pictures, and have another author write the text.

Falconer wasn't pleased. "I'd made this character and this story, and I really didn't want it to be 'illustrated by Ian Falconer'," he said. Then, he got a call from an editor at a children's book publisher. She'd seen his *New Yorker* illustrations and wanted to know if he'd like to do a children's book. "And I had *Olivia,*" recalls Falconer. The book was an instant success.

OLIVIA: As her many fans know, Olivia is a delightful, energetic pig. So energetic, in fact, that she wears people out. The book features Olivia busy with all the things she loves. She dresses up (her bright red clothes are scattered across the book's opening pages). She builds a sand castle (that looks like the Empire State Building). She goes to the museum (and imagines herself as a dancer in a Degas painting). Finally, Olivia goes to sleep (dreaming of becoming an opera star).

Olivia quickly became a book loved by children and adults, too. It won many awards, including a Caldecott Honor. That's one of the most important awards in children's books. *Olivia* was also translated into 17 languages. And it brought a steady income to Ian Falconer. "After all these years painting and working for nonprofit theater, it's nice to have some money," he says.

Falconer says he was "completely overwhelmed" by *Olivia*'s success. Soon he was at work on another book featuring the amazing pig.

OLIVIA SAVES THE CIRCUS: Olivia returned in *Olivia Saves the Circus*. In this book, Olivia tells her class what she did on her summer vacation. And, Olivia being Olivia, it's quite a tale.

Olivia, her mother, and brother go to the circus. But when they get there, all the circus performers are out with ear infections! Olivia saves the day, taming lions, walking the tightrope, and floating through the air on the trapeze. When she gets to the end of her story, her

teacher asks her if it's true. "To the best of my recollection," claims Olivia.

Young readers loved the second *Olivia* book. Like the first, it features Falconer's beautiful black-and-white

charcoal drawings, with highlights of bright red and salmon pink.

Falconer has also produced two board books for the youngest readers. In *Olivia Counts* and *Olivia's Opposites* toddlers learn about counting and opposites.

FUTURE PLANS: Falconer's next book featuring Olivia comes out in Fall 2003. It's called *Olivia and the Missing Toy.* Falconer is also continuing to design sets and costumes for ballets and operas.

IAN FALCONER'S HOME AND FAMILY: Falconer, who isn't married, lives in New York City. He still enjoys visiting the real Olivia and her family.

QUOTE

What did the real Olivia do when presented with the book named for her?

"She took it in stride, as though it was perfectly natural for someone to write a book about her. She took the book to class and read it aloud to her classmates. She even autographed it for them."

SOME BOOKS BY IAN FALCONER:

Olivia
Olivia Saves the Circus
Olivia Counts
Olivia's Opposites
Olivia and the Missing Toy

FOR MORE INFORMATION ABOUT IAN FALCONER:

Write: Atheneum Books for Young Readers
Simon & Schuster Children's Publishing
1230 Avenue of the Americas
New York, New York 10020

WORLD WIDE WEB SITE:

http://www.simonsays.com

Mary GrandPré

1954-
American Artist and Illustrator
Illustrator of the *Harry Potter* Books

MARY GRANDPRÉ WAS BORN on February 13, 1954, in
South Dakota. Her last name is pronounced "grand pray."
Very little information is available about her early life,
including facts about her family. Mary moved to
Minnesota when she was two.

MARY GRANDPRÉ GREW UP loving to draw. "I've been drawing since I was five years old," she says. She loved to study and imitate the work of other artists, too. "I used to stink up the house with oil paints," she says.

When she was about 10, she tried to paint like Salvador Dali. He was a 20th-century painter known for his strange but fascinating art. "I liked the way he stretched things," recalls GrandPré. "He made them real, but weird."

She also liked to copy black-and-white photos out of books. "I must have been bored," she says. "But to me it was fun. I loved the colors of black and white." Even though she worked with oils and other paints, her favorite art material was, and is, pastels. She still uses them for her work.

MARY GRANDPRÉ WENT TO SCHOOL at the local public schools in Minnesota. When she was in her mid-20s, she went to art school. She attended the Minneapolis College of Art & Design. There, she studied both painting and illustrating. She learned that she loved to do both.

GrandPré didn't start working in art right after graduating from college. She had an art portfolio that she took to ad agencies and other places to sell her work.

For a few years, she worked as a waitress to support herself. But she kept working on her art. She began to develop her own artistic style. She calls it "soft geometry." By that, she means a soft-edged look, colored in pastels. "I've always drawn with pastels," she says. "I've tried other things. But I always finish up with pastels."

STARTING TO WORK AS AN ARTIST: GrandPré's first art jobs were doing ads for stores and magazines. Then she began to get work as an illustrator.

BECOMING AN ILLUSTRATOR: GrandPré started to illustrate picture books in the 1990s. One of those early books is *Chin Yu Min and the Ginger Cat*. The book is a retelling of an ancient Chinese folktale. GrandPré's rich and warm drawings help tell the story of an old woman and the cat who brings her good fortune.

HARRY POTTER: In 1996, GrandPré got a call from Scholastic books. They were publishing the American edition of a book called *Harry Potter and the Sorcerer's Stone*. It was by an unknown author named J.K. Rowling. They needed a cover and some interior illustrations.

"It sounded like a nice job, so I said 'sure'," recalls GrandPré. She read through the book, and was delighted. She loved the "magic of the story and of the characters." She said it was "not only easy but exciting" to illustrate the book, because "Rowling's writing is so vivid." She sent three covers, and Scholastic chose one.

"They were great to work with," she says. "I think I remember them saying there might be more. At the time, it just seemed like another job."

As everyone knows, it was anything but another job.
To date, the five Harry Potter volumes have sold millions

of copies around the world. The books sold in England are illustrated by another artist, but GrandPré's illustrations appear in books sold in the U.S. and many nations. Needless to say, their success has made her famous.

WORKING ON THE HARRY POTTER BOOKS: GrandPré gets the books several months before they're published. She reads them, then thinks about what she'll draw. She can't tell anyone — even her family — what the new books are about. It has to stay a secret.

It takes her about two months to create the cover and illustrations. "Two weeks for notes taken from the book, then two weeks for preliminary sketches. One week to review the cover, two weeks for the final cover," she says.

When she first drew Harry, GrandPré actually used herself as the model. If you look at her picture and Harry you can see the similarities. She used other models for other characters. "My dog Chopper, I believe, is somehow related to Hagrid," she says.

How does it feel to have created the image of such a popular character? "It's pretty cool," says GrandPré. "It's great to see kids being able to relate and show interest in reading and also the drawing. I'm very proud to be a part of the books, as they will sit on the shelves as classics for years to come."

GrandPré met J.K. Rowling a few years ago. They had dinner in Chicago, where Rowling praised her illustrations. "She told me my covers are her favorite," says the artist.

OTHER ART WORK: As much as GrandPré enjoys drawing Harry, she also likes doing other art work. "Harry Potter is the most popular part of my work," she says.

"But it's a very small part." She continues to illustrate for other authors. Some of these books are for adults, and some are for children. Among the children's books she's illustrated are *Aunt Claire's Yellow Beehive Hair* and *Plum*.

For GrandPré, each illustration job presents a particular "problem" to be solved. "No technique should be bigger or more important than the problem the illustration needs to solve. Good composition, good color, good drawing, combined with a strong concept can enable you to work on anything."

ANTZ: GrandPré has not worked on the Harry Potter movies, but she has done illustrations for other films. In 1998, she created background landscapes for the movie *Antz*. She loved the challenge of looking at the world through an insect's eye. She recalls "the great fun of looking at ordinary things through a magnifying glass, and really being appreciated for being an artist." She also worked on the film *Ice Age*.

GrandPré also does ads and other commercial work. She did a series of posters for the Land's End catalog a few years ago. The profits went to an organization that buys books for poor children.

FUTURE PLANS: GrandPré is planning to write and illustrate a children's book of her own. "I'm not sure when the book will actually be written," she says. "But I already

have ideas written down for stories now. I want to create books that speak to people of all ages." She has two more Harry Potter books to do. Then, she's looking forward to her own work. "I'd like more personal time in the studio to grow as an artist. I just want to keep making art — wherever it takes me."

MARY GRANDPRÉ'S HOME AND FAMILY: GrandPré lives in St. Paul, Minnesota, with her husband, Tom Casmer, and three stepchildren. She works in a studio in her home. When she's not working, she likes to cook and work on old houses. She has two dogs, Charlie and Chopper, and a cat, Jasper Cumulonimbus Cloud.

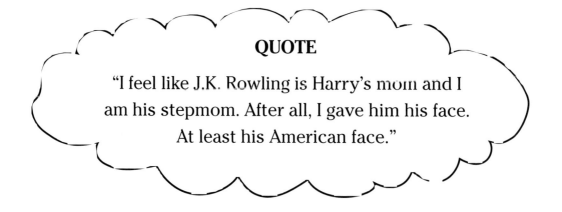

QUOTE

"I feel like J.K. Rowling is Harry's mom and I am his stepmom. After all, I gave him his face. At least his American face."

SOME OF MARY GRANDPRÉ'S ILLUSTRATED BOOKS:

The *Harry Potter* Books:

Harry Potter and the Sorcerer's Stone
Harry Potter and the Chamber of Secrets
Harry Potter and the Prisoner of Azkaban
Harry Potter and the Goblet of Fire
Harry Potter and the Order of the Phoenix

Others:

Chin Yu Min and the Ginger Cat
The Vegetables Go to Bed
Batwings and the Curtain of Night
The House of Wisdom
Aunt Claire's Yellow Beehive Hair
The Sea Chest
Plum

FOR MORE INFORMATION ABOUT MARY GRANDPRÉ:

Write: Scholastic Books
557 Broadway
New York, NY 10012

WORLD WIDE WEB SITES:

http://www.marygrandpre.org
http://www.scholastic.com/harrypotter/books/illustrator

Robert McCloskey

1914-2003
American Children's Author and Illustrator
Creator of *Make Way for Ducklings, Time of Wonder,* and *Blueberries for Sal*

ROBERT McCLOSKEY WAS BORN on September 15, 1914, in Hamilton, Ohio. His parents were Howard and Mabel McCloskey.

ROBERT McCLOSKEY GREW UP in Hamilton, a small town in Ohio. He was an active, curious boy. From a very early age, he loved music. "From the time my fingers were long enough to play the scale, I took piano lessons," he remembered. "I started next to play the harmonica, the drums, and then the oboe. The musician's life was the life for me."

But then curious Bob McCloskey turned his energy to invention. "I collected old electric motors, bits of wire, and old clocks," he recalled. "I built trains and cranes with remote controls." Soon, his house was full of his inventions. "My family's Christmas trees revolved, lights flashed and buzzers buzzed, fuses blew and sparks flew. The inventor's life was the life for me. That is, until I started making drawings for the high school annual (yearbook)."

ROBERT McCLOSKEY WENT TO SCHOOL at the public schools in Hamilton. In high school, he made drawings for the school paper and yearbook. He was a fine artist, and he won a scholarship to an art college in Boston.

McCloskey moved to Boston in 1932, where he attended Vesper George School of Art. Every day, he walked through the Public Garden on his way to class. He often stopped to watch the ducks that lived there. He would return to his memory of them in his most famous book.

After two years in Boston, McCloskey moved to New York City. There, he attended the National Academy of

Design. By 1938, he was ready to try to make his living as an artist.

BECOMING AN ARTIST: McCloskey spent two summers painting on Cape Cod, in Massachusetts. But he had a hard time selling enough paintings to make a living.

Back in New York, McCloskey took his artwork to a children's publisher. The editor there reviewed his work. "She looked at the examples of 'great art' that I had brought along," he remembered. She gently encouraged him to put away his drawings of dragons and landscapes. She thought he should concentrate on his childhood memories of Ohio.

STARTING TO WRITE AND DRAW FOR CHILDREN: McCloskey returned to Ohio. Soon, he was drawing pictures from his youth. Then he wrote the text to go with the drawings. They became his first book, *Lentil*. Published in 1941, the book tells the story of a young boy growing up in a small town, who learns to play the harmonica.

Having his first book published was a great thrill for McCloskey. "It was as though I was sort of tied up in a paper bag or gunny sack with a rope around the neck of it. All of a sudden with the acceptance of that first book everything sort of spilled out!"

MAKE WAY FOR DUCKLINGS: McCloskey's next book was *Make Way for Ducklings.* It tells the story of Mr. and

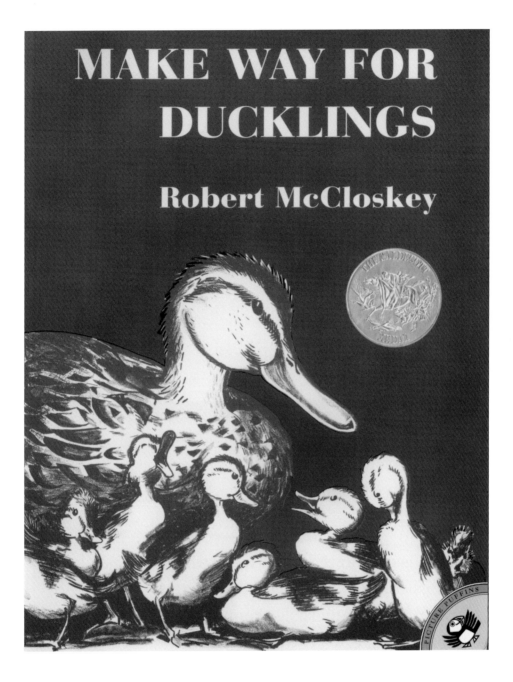

Mrs. Mallard and their eight ducklings. The parents must find a way for their little ones to make their way through the busy city of Boston.

An inner page from Make Way for Ducklings.

The ducklings — Jack, Kack, Lack, Mack, Nack, Ouack, Pack, and Quack — are guided by their mother across crowded streets. Kindly Officer Michael makes sure the traffic stops to let the ducks pass safely. As the story ends, the family reaches its home in the Public Garden.

McCloskey wanted to make sure he drew the ducklings correctly. So, before he started the book, he bought four baby ducks. He kept them in his studio, and sketched them as they waddled on the floor. He put them in the bathtub, and sketched them as they swam.

He obviously got them right. *Make Way for Ducklings* has been a favorite with children for more than 60 years. It has sold millions of copies in several languages. And it inspired an artist named Nancy Schoen to create a sculpture of the duck family. It's in Boston's Public Gardens, where children play on it every day.

BLUEBERRIES FOR SAL: McCloskey's next book is set in Maine. It features little Sal, who is picking blueberries with her mom. Nearby, a mother bear and her cub are also looking for berries. Sal and the cub somehow get mixed up, and they start following each other's mom. All turns out all right in the end, and Sal and the cub find their own mothers.

Sal is based on McCloskey's daughter Sarah, called Sal. She appears in several of his books, including *One Morning in Maine.* The McCloskey family lived in Maine for many years. The beauty of the land inspired many of McCloskey's most beloved books, including *Time of Wonder.*

TIME OF WONDER: *Time of Wonder* is set on an island in Penobscot Bay in Maine. It tells the story of a summer spent in a beautiful setting. McCloskey used watercolors for his illustrations. He paints a picture of the water, the land, and the people of Maine.

OTHER WORKS: McCloskey wrote two books for older readers. *Homer Price* and *Centerberg Tales* feature the adventures of the feisty Homer.

McCloskey wrote and illustrated just eight books. "I have to wait until it bubbles out," he said about creating his works. He always took his time to get the words and pictures just right. "It's a good feeling to be able to put down a line and know that it's right," he said. He also illustrated books for other authors, including a series featuring a character named Henry Reed.

McCloskey's books won several major awards. *Make Way for Ducklings* and *Time of Wonder* won the Caldecott Medal. That is one of the most important awards in children's literature. *Blueberries for Sal* and *One Morning in Maine* were Caldecott Honor books.

ON ART: McCloskey was a great supporter of artists and the importance of art. "It is important that we develop people who can make worthwhile pictures. It is important that we teach people to 'read' these pictures. That is why, in my opinion, every child, along with learning to read and write, should be taught to draw and design."

ROBERT McCLOSKEY'S HOME AND FAMILY: McCloskey married Margaret Durand in 1940. She was a children's librarian and the daughter of a children's author. The McCloskeys had two daughters, Sarah (called Sal) and Jane. Sal and Jane became characters in McCloskey's later books.

The family lived for many years on Deer Isle in Maine. McCloskey died at his home on Deer Isle on June 30, 2003. He was 88 years old. He is remembered as the beloved creator of books like *Make Way for Ducklings.* They have been treasured for generations, and will be for years to come.

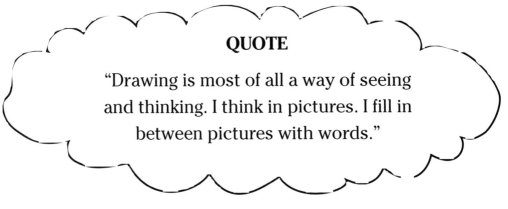

QUOTE

"Drawing is most of all a way of seeing and thinking. I think in pictures. I fill in between pictures with words."

SOME OF ROBERT McCLOSKEY'S BOOKS:

As Author and Illustrator:
Lentil
Make Way for Ducklings

Homer Price
Blueberries for Sal
Centerburg Tales
One Morning in Maine
Time of Wonder
*Burt Dow, Deep-Water Man: A Tale of the Sea in
  the Classic Tradition*

As Illustrator:

Yankee Doodle's Cousins
Tree Toad
Journey Cake, HO!
Henry Reed, Inc.
Henry Reed's Big Show

FOR MORE INFORMATION ABOUT ROBERT McCLOSKEY:

Write: Penguin USA
345 Hudson Street
New York, NY 10014

WORLD WIDE WEB SITES:

http://www.hbook.com/obit_mccloskey.shtml
http://www.penguinputnam.com

Ichiro Suzuki

1973-
Japanese Professional Baseball Player
with the Seattle Mariners

ICHIRO SUZUKI WAS BORN on October 22, 1973, in Kasugai, Japan. His name is pronounced EE-chee-row sue-ZOO-key. He prefers to be called by his first name only.

ICHIRO SUZUKI GREW UP in Nagoya, Japan. By the age of three, he was playing baseball. His dad practiced with him every day.

By the time Ichiro was in elementary school, he was playing every day. He had the same dedication he has today. He spent hours hitting, pitching, and fielding.

ICHIRO SUZUKI WENT TO SCHOOL at the local schools in Nagoya. He especially liked social studies. He loved sports and was a star baseball player for his high school team. He graduated from Aikoudai Meiden High School in 1992. He didn't go to college. Instead, he went right into the pros.

STARTING TO PLAY PRO BASEBALL: Ichiro began to play pro baseball right out of high school. He spent nine seasons with the Orix Blue Wave, a team in Japan's Pacific League. Ichiro was a superstar. He won seven batting titles and Gold Gloves. He was named MVP three times. And he lost all his privacy.

Baseball is incredibly popular in Japan. Star players like Ichiro are as famous as rock stars. He couldn't go anywhere without being mobbed by fans. Fans and photographers followed him everywhere. "They would even watch me go to the haircut place or the restaurant," he recalls. "Then they would interview the people at the hair cutters." When he got married, he chose to have the wedding in Los Angeles, to avoid fans.

Ichiro makes a catch in the outfield.

COMING TO THE UNITED STATES: In 2000, Ichiro decided he needed more of a challenge. "It wasn't interesting any more," he says. "As the better pitchers left my league, it wasn't fun." Great Japanese pitchers like Hideo Nomo had moved to the U.S. He thought it was time for him to move, too.

PLAYING FOR THE SEATTLE MARINERS: Ichiro had played with the Seattle Mariners during spring training in 1999. They saw him play, and they were interested. The

Mariners paid the Blue Wave $13 million just to talk to Ichiro about coming to Seattle. On November 18, 2000, he made the move. He signed a $15 million contract to play for the Mariners. He was the first Japanese non-pitcher to ever play in Major League Baseball.

ROOKIE SEASON: No one was sure just how Ichiro would work out in American pro baseball. He'd faced the toughest pitchers in Japan. Now he would face the best pitchers in the world.

In that first season, Ichiro showed what he could do. He took over right field, where he throws right-handed. Then the left-handed slugger took over the batting box. By the end of his rookie year, he led the major leagues in key stats. He topped the league in batting, with a .350 average. He led all others in hits, with 242. And he stole more bases than any other player, with 56. He also led the Mariners to the 2001 American League division title.

Ichiro's rookie season won him two major awards. He was named Rookie of the Year for the American League, as well as Most Valuable Player (MVP). He accepted the awards humbly. "I cannot be a regular, ordinary player anymore. I just need to play to make fans happy — make my team, maybe opposing teams, enjoy my play."

His fellow players had nothing but praise for him. "He's one of the best players in the league, hands down,"

said Yankee Jason Giambi. His fellow Mariners call him "Wizard" for his incredible ability. "It's very simple," says Mariner Mike Cameron. "Time and time again, Ichiro has been our go-to guy. He hits, we win."

The fans took notice, too. Ichiro was named to the 2001 All-Star team with 3.3 million votes. That's more than anyone else received. He became "Ichiro" to his new fans. He's the only player to have his first name on his jersey.

THE 2002 SEASON: Ichiro had an outstanding season in 2002. He showed that his rookie year was just a sample of what he could do. He placed second in overall hits, fourth in batting, and fourth in stolen bases. He also became the first Mariner to get more than 200 hits in one season.

Ichiro has a special routine he follows during each game. When he gets to the outfield, he does stretching exercises. When he gets to the plate, he follows a series of moves to get ready to bat. "Some people may think it's strange," he says. "But if something works, there's no need to change it."

After games, he rubs his feet with a special wooden stick. And he spends time after each game oiling his glove. He talks about how important it is to focus. "The idea is to always make sure you're in a normal mental state," he says. That concentration is just part of how he

prepares. He also makes sure he eats right, gets enough sleep, and follows a careful conditioning plan.

THE 2003 SEASON: So far, the 2003 season has been a great one for Ichiro. By the All-Star break in mid-July, he was on a pace to break more records. And he was selected again for the All-Star game, with over 2 million votes, more than any other player. He scored the American League's first run in the game. That helped them beat the National League, 7-6.

Ichiro is a great all-around player. He can hit all kinds of pitches. It's hard for pitchers to figure out how to throw to him. And he has incredible speed. He can make it to first base in just 3.7 seconds. He uses that speed to steal bases in record-breaking numbers. In the outfield, he catches impossible drives, and he throws with lightning speed to get players out.

Ichiro loves playing in the U.S. He says the best thing about it is "the fans. I like the attitude they take to base-ball." He also loves hot dogs and pizza.

Ichiro is still learning English, but he's picked up a few phrases. He often greets fellow players with "Wassup?" and "Thanks, dawg." He's known for his cool wrap-around sunglasses and wispy sideburns.

The hard-working Ichiro has some big plans for his team. "One of our goals is to get to the World Series. Of

Ichiro signs autographs for fans.

course, we have a lot of things day-to-day we have to take care of first. We can't dwell on an end result without taking care of business." But after the All-Star victory, Ichiro thought they might be on their way. "I started to get a feeling that we'd like to play the World Series in Seattle," he said.

ICHIRO SUZUKI'S HOME AND FAMILY: Ichiro is married to Yumiko Fukushima, a former TV host in Japan. They have a home in the Seattle suburb of Bellevue. They also have a home in Kobe, Japan, where they live in the off-season. In his spare time, Ichiro likes to golf.

QUOTE

"I will never regret the fact that I came
over here and tried to play in America.
Because I have had that dream and made that
dream come true, I have no regrets. I am
making my dream come true."

SOME OF ICHIRO SUZUKI'S RECORDS:

Rookie of the Year, American League: 2001
Most Valuable Player, American League: 2001
All-Star Team: 2001-2003

FOR MORE INFORMATION ABOUT ICHIRO SUZUKI:

Write: Ichiro Suzuki
c/o Seattle Mariners Baseball Club
P.O. Box 4100
Seattle, WA 98104

WORLD WIDE WEB SITES:

http://www.mlb.com
http://seattlemariners.com

Serena Williams

1981-
American Professional Tennis Player
Ranked #1 in the World

SERENA WILLIAMS WAS BORN on September 26, 1981, in Saginaw, Michigan. Her parents are Richard Williams and Oracene Price. When Serena was growing up, her father ran his own security business. Her mother was a nurse. Now, they manage Serena's career.

Serena is the youngest of five girls. Her sisters are Yetunde, Isha, Lyndrea, and Venus. Like Serena, Venus is a top professional tennis player. The other Williams sisters do not play pro tennis. Instead, they have careers in other areas.

Serena has always been especially close to Venus, who is just 15 months older. When she was little, Serena copied everything her sister did. "There were two Venus Williamses in our family," she recalls. "It was crazy." "It was tough for me to stop being Venus and become the person I am," says Serena. But finally, she realized she had to be herself. "I just said to myself, 'I'm not Venus. I'm Serena'."

SERENA WILLIAMS GREW UP in Compton, California. Her father had decided before she was born that she and her sisters would learn to play tennis. He had seen a tennis tournament on TV where a player won $30,000. He decided to learn the game.

Richard Williams had never played tennis. He bought books and videos and taught himself. Then he taught all the girls to play.

STARTING TO PLAY TENNIS: Serena began to play when she was just four years old. She played on the city courts in Compton, a rough neighborhood outside of Los

Venus (left) and Serena (right) after winning Olympic gold medals in doubles tennis, September 2000.

Angeles. Even though the courts were cracked and full of weeds, she played every day.

Soon, it was clear that Venus and Serena had natural talent for the game. "I taught my children, that they were the very best," Richard recalls. "And they believed it."

Serena played in her first tournament when she was nine. Soon, she was one of the best young players in California. But her father was concerned about all the attention Serena and Venus received. He wanted them to have normal childhoods. So he decided they wouldn't compete for several years.

When Serena was ten, the family moved to Florida. There, Serena and Venus trained under the watchful eye of their father. And they got better and better.

SERENA WILLIAMS WENT TO SCHOOL at home. Their mother has a teaching degree, and she home schooled the girls until high school. Serena attended a private school, Driftwood Academy, for high school. She graduated in 1998.

PLAYING PROFESSIONAL TENNIS: By the time she graduated, Serena had been playing pro tennis for three years. She played her first professional match at 14. She lost by a score of 6-1, 6-1.

HOW TENNIS IS SCORED: Here is what those numbers mean. In women's tennis, a player wins a "match" by defeating her opponent in 2 out of 3 "sets." The first player to win six games usually wins the set. If she doesn't win by at least two games, the set is decided by a tie-breaker. So, in Serena's first match, the winner won both sets by a score of 6 games to 1.

Serena didn't play another match for more than a year. Instead, she worked on her game. She joined the Women's Tennis Association (WTA) tour in 1997. She was ready to take on the best pros in the world.

ON THE WTA TOUR: Serena entered her first WTA tournament ranked 304th. That year, she beat the fourth and seventh-ranked players in the world. She moved up in the rankings, to Number 102.

In 1998, she beat the second-ranked player, Lindsey Davenport. By the end of the year, she'd moved up to Number 30. That allowed her to take part in "Grand Slam" events.

THE GRAND SLAM: The "Grand Slam" is the name of the four biggest matches in tennis. They are the U.S. Open, the French Open, the Australian Open, and Wimbledon.

Serena's first Grand Slam match was at the 1999 Australian Open. She won her first match against the 10th-ranked player in the world. She'd defeated five Top 10 players faster than anyone in the history of women's tennis. Then, she lost her next match to another great player, her sister Venus.

PLAYING AGAINST VENUS: In all her years in tennis, one of Serena's toughest opponents has been Venus. "When we were younger, it was difficult for me to play Venus," says Serena. "She'd always beat me so badly I had to

Serena (left) and Venus (right) in the Wimbledon ladies doubles match, June 2003.

improve just so I could stay in the game. Even now when we practice together I have to watch out because she'll just blow me off the court."

Serena (left) and Venus (right), with trophies, after the Wimbledon singles final, July 2003.

Yet even though they compete against each other in almost every tournament, they remain best friends. "Family comes first, no matter how many times we play each other," says Serena. "Nothing will come between me and my sister."

The 1999 season was a terrific one for Serena. She won her first WTA championship in France. Then she won the U.S. Open. It was her first Grand Slam win. She was the first African-American woman to win the championship since Althea Gibson in 1958. And she and Venus won the women's doubles title, too. (In doubles tennis, teams of two players each play against one another.)

Serena also beat her sister for the first time in 1999. She and Venus faced each other in the final for the Grand Slam Cup. After that win, Serena moved up to Number Four in the rankings.

In 2000, Serena won three championships and faced Venus in the semifinals at Wimbledon. She lost to Venus in that match. But the two continued to be a major power in doubles tennis. That year, they won the Wimbledon doubles title.

THE OLYMPICS: In Fall 2000, Serena and Venus became the first sisters to win an Olympic gold medal in tennis. They won the final in women's doubles. After their win, they threw their rackets in the air and screamed with delight. The match was the 22nd win in a row for the doubles team of Serena and Venus.

In 2001, Serena reached the quarter finals in the Australian and French Opens and at Wimbledon. In the fall, she faced Venus for the U.S. Open championship. Venus won that year.

The 2002 season was a great one for Serena. She was ranked Number One in the world. She won three Grand Slam events: The French Open, Wimbledon, and the U.S.

Open. She was strong and at the top of her game. Her powerful serves reached 115 miles per hour. She had strength and endurance. She was the player to beat.

In Spring 2003, still ranked Number One, Serena won the Australian Open. She had now won all four Grand Slam titles. A few months later, Serena lost in the semi-final of the French Open.

Then, in July, she was back at Wimbledon. In the final, she faced her sister Venus. Venus was battling an injury, but she played with great strength and heart. Serena was concerned about her sister, but she tried to stay focused on the match. "I just had to tell myself to look at the ball and nothing else," she said. In great form, she beat Venus to win Wimbledon again.

After her great Wimbledon win, Serena received the 2003 ESPY Award as Female Athlete of the Year.

LIFE OUTSIDE OF TENNIS: Serena has a very active life outside the world of tennis. She likes to design and wear her own clothes. In fact, she and Venus have their own line of clothing. She also has several endorsement contracts for tennis products and clothing.

Serena also likes to act. She (and Venus) appeared as guest voices on an episode of "The Simpsons." She also appeared in a music video and in the movie *Black Knight*. In 2002, she was on an episode of "My Wife and Kids."

Another important part of Serena's life is religion. She and her family are Jehovah's Witnesses. Serena says it gives her a "strong spiritual background."

SERENA WILLIAMS'S HOME AND FAMILY: Serena is single and shares a home with Venus in Florida. It is a large mansion, which they enjoyed decorating them-selves. They have tennis courts and a pool. They also have two dogs, a Yorkie and a pit bull.

Both Serena and Venus do a lot of charity work. They give tennis clinics in poor neighborhoods. They also encourage African-American kids to get involved in tennis. "Let's face it, there are not many black people in this sport," she says. "Black people are definitely going to look at me and say I want to be like her. But a lot of other people do that, too."

Her hobbies include reading, watching movies, and listening to music. She especially likes Brandy and Mariah Carey.

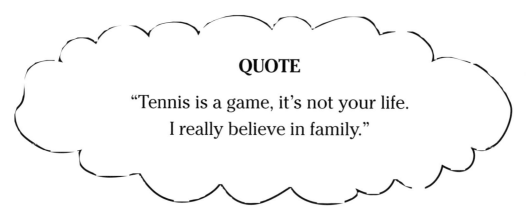

QUOTE

"Tennis is a game, it's not your life.
I really believe in family."

SOME OF SERENA WILLIAMS'S RECORDS:

Australian Open: Singles Champion, 2003

French Open: Doubles Champion (with Venus Williams), 1999; Singles Champion, 2002

Olympic Tennis: Doubles Champion (with Venus Williams), 2000

U.S. Open: Singles Champion, 1999, 2002; Doubles Champion (with Venus Williams): 1999, 2002

Wimbledon: Singles Champion: 2002, 2003

FOR MORE INFORMATION ABOUT SERENA WILLIAMS:

Write: WTA
One Progress Plaza
Suite 1500
St. Petersburg, FL 33701

WORLD WIDE WEB SITE:

http://www.wtatour.com

Photo and Illustrations Credits

Ben Carson/Photos: Courtesy Johns Hopkins/© Keith Weller Photography; AP/Wide World Photos. Cover: GIFTED HANDS/Zondervan Publishing House

Richard Cheney/Photos: DaviBohrer/Courtesy Office of the Vice President; AP/Wide World Photos; Reuters/Landov; AP/Wide World Photos.

Linda Ellerbee/Photos: Newscom.com; Courtesy of "Nick News." Cover: GIRL REPORTER BLOWS LID OFF TOWN! (HarperCollins Publisher) Jacket and author photographs © 2000 by Gordon Munro. Jacket © 2000 by HarperCollins Publisher.

Ian Falconer/Photos: Roddy McDowell. Covers:OLIVIA (An Anne Schwartz Book. Atheneum Books for Young Readers. Simon & Schuster.) Jacket illustration copyright © 2000 by Ian Falconer; OLIVIA SAVES THE CIRCUS (An Anne Schwartz Book. Atheneum Books for Young Readers. Simon & Schuster.) Jacket illustration copyright © 2000 by Ian Falconer; OLIVIA COUNTS (Atheneum Books for Young Readers. An imprint of Simon & Schuster Children's Publishing Division.) Copyright © 2002 by Ian Falconer; OLIVIA'S OPPOSITES (Atheneum Books for Young Readers. An imprint of Simon & Schuster Children's Publishing Division.) Copyright © 2002 by Ian Falconer; OLIVIA AND THE MISSING TOY (Atheneum Books for Young Readers. An imprint of Simon & Schuster Children's Publishing Division.) Copyright © 2003 by Ian Falconer.

Mary GrandPré/Photo: Newscom.com. Covers:HARRY POTTER AND THE SORCERER'S STONE jacket art copyright © 1998 by Mary GrandPré. Jacket design by Mary GrandPré and David Saylor; HARRY POTTER AND THE CHAMBER OF SECRETS and HARRY POTTER AND THE PRISONER OF AZKABAN jacket art copyright © 1999 by Mary GrandPré. Jacket design by Mary GrandPré and David Saylor; HARRY POTTER AND THE GOBLET OF FIRE jacket art copyright © 2000 by Mary GrandPré. Jacket design by Mary GrandPré and David Saylor; HARRY POTTER AND THE ORDER OF THE PHOENIX jacket art by Mary GrandPré © 2003 Warner Bros. Jacket design by Mary GrandPré and David Saylor; PLUM (Scholastic) Illustrated by Mary GrandPré.

Robert McCloskey/Photo: Elaine S. Martens. Covers: MAKE WAY FOR DUCKLINGS (Puffin Books), Copyright © Robert McCloskey, 1941. Copyright renewed © Robert McCloskey, 1969; BLUEBERRIES FOR SAL (Puffin Books), Copyright © Robert McCloskey, 1948. Copyright renewed © Robert McCloskey, 1976; TIME OF WONDER (Puffin Books), Copyright © Robert McCloskey, 1957. Copyright renewed © Robert McCloskey, 1985.

Ichiro Suzuki/Photos: Courtesy of Seattle Mariners. Time Life Pictures/Getty Images; AP/Wide Word Photos. Back Cover: Ben Van Houten/Seattle Mariners

Serena Williams/Photos: AP/Wide World Photos (pages 79, 82, and 86); Newscom.com (pages 81 and 88); Thomas Coex/AFP/Getty Images (page 85).

Name Index

Listed below are the names of all individuals who have appeared in *Biography for Beginners,* followed by the issue and year in which they appear.

Subject Index

This index includes subjects, occupations, and ethnic and minority origins for individuals who have appeared in *Biography for Beginners.*

farmer

Bentley, Wilson
"Snowflake"

female

Aguilera, Christina,
Spring 2001

Aliki, Spring '96

Applegate, K.A.,
Spring 2000

Berenstain, Jan, Fall '95

Blair, Bonnie, Spring '95

Blume, Judy, Fall '95

Brandy, Fall '96

Brett, Jan, Spring '95

Bunting, Eve, Fall 2001

Burton, Virginia Lee,
Spring '97

Bush, Laura, Spring 2002

Butcher, Susan, Fall 2000

Byars, Betsy, Fall 2002

Cannon, Janell, Spring '99

Cleary, Beverly, Spring '95

Clinton, Chelsea, Fall '96

Clinton, Hillary, Spring '96

Cole, Joanna, Fall '95

Cooney, Barbara,
Spring 2001

Danziger, Paula, Fall 2001

Duff, Hilary, Spring 2003

Earle, Sylvia, Fall '99

Ehlert, Lois, Fall 2000

Ellerbee, Linda, Fall 2003

Estefan, Gloria, Spring '96

Giff, Patricia Reilly,
Spring 2001

Ginsburg, Ruth Bader,
Fall 2000

Goodall, Jane, Spring '96

GrandPré, Mary, Fall 2003

Hamilton, Virginia, Fall '99

Hamm, Mia, Spring '98

Hart, Melissa Joan, Fall '95

Houston, Whitney,
Spring '98

Jemison, Mae, Fall '96

Jones, Marion, Spring 2001

Joyner-Kersee, Jackie,
Fall '95

Kerrigan, Nancy, Fall '95

Kwan, Michelle,
Spring 2002

Lewis, Shari, Spring '99

Lin, Maya, Spring 2001

Lindgren, Astrid, Fall 2002

Lipinski, Tara, Spring '98

Lucid, Shannon, Fall '97

MacLachlan, Patricia,
Spring 2003

Martin, Ann M., Spring '96

McKissack, Patricia, Fall '98

Miller, Shannon, Spring '95

Moceanu, Dominique,
Fall '98

Japanese
Suzuki, Ichiro, Fall 2003

journalist
Ellerbee, Linda, Fall 2003

judge
Ginsburg, Ruth Bader,
Fall 2000

musicians
Aguilera, Christina,
Spring 2001
Estefan, Gloria, Spring '96
Houston, Whitney,
Spring '98
Ma, Yo-Yo, Spring '96
Marsalis, Wynton,
Spring '99
Perlman, Yitzhak,
Spring '98
mith, Will, Fall 2000

**National Security Adviser
to the President of the
United States**
Rice, Condoleezza,
Spring 2002

naturalist
Irwin, Steve, Spring 2003

oceanographer
Ballard, Robert, Fall 2002
Earle, Sylvia, Fall '99

Olympics
Armstrong, Lance, Fall 2002
Blair, Bonnie, Spring '95
Carter, Vince, Fall 2001
Hamm, Mia, Spring '98
Hill, Grant, Fall '97
Jones, Marion, Spring 2001
Jordan, Michael, Spring '97
Joyner-Kersee, Jackie,
Fall '95
Kerrigan, Nancy, Fall '95
Kwan, Michelle,
Spring 2002
Lipinski, Tara, Spring '98
Miller, Shannon,
Spring '95
Moceanu, Dominique,
Fall '98
Robinson, David, Fall '96
Scurry, Briana, Fall '99
Strug, Kerri, Spring '97
Swoopes, Sheryl,
Spring 2000
Van Dyken, Amy,
Spring 2000
Williams, Serena, Fall 2003
Yamaguchi, Kristi,
Fall '97

Birthday Index

January
12 John Lasseter (1957)
14 Shannon Lucid (1943)
17 Shari Lewis (1934)
21 Hakeem Olajuwon (1963)
26 Vince Carter (1977)
28 Wayne Gretzky (1961)
29 Bill Peet (1915)
Rosemary Wells (1943)
Oprah Winfrey (1954)
30 Dick Cheney (1941)

February
4 Rosa Parks (1913)
7 Laura Ingalls Wilder (1867)
9 Wilson "Snowflake" Bentley (1865)
11 Jane Yolen (1939)
Brandy (1979)
12 Judy Blume (1938)
David Small (1945)
13 Mary GrandPré (1954)
15 Norman Bridwell (1928)
Amy Van Dyken (1973)
16 LeVar Burton (1957)
17 Michael Jordan (1963)
22 Steve Irwin (1962)
27 Chelsea Clinton (1980)

March
2 Dr. Seuss (1904)
David Satcher (1941)
3 Patricia MacLachlan (1938)
Jackie Joyner-Kersee (1962)
4 Garrett Morgan (1877)
Dav Pilkey (1966)
5 Jake Lloyd (1989)
10 Shannon Miller (1977)
11 Ezra Jack Keats (1916)
12 Virginia Hamilton (1936)
15 Ruth Bader Ginsburg (1933)
16 Shaquille O'Neal (1972)
17 Mia Hamm (1972)
18 Bonnie Blair (1964)
20 Fred Rogers (1928)
Louis Sachar (1954)
21 Rosie O'Donnell (1962)
25 Sheryl Swoopes (1971)
31 Al Gore (1948)

April
3 Jane Goodall (1934)
5 Colin Powell (1937)
8 Kofi Annan (1938)

April (continued)

12 Beverly Cleary (1916)
 Tony Hawk (1968)
16 Garth Williams (1912)
18 Melissa Joan Hart
 (1976)
26 Patricia Reilly Giff
 (1935)
27 Barbara Park (1947)

May

 4 Don Wood (1945)
10 Leo Lionni (1910)
 Christopher Paul
 Curtis (1953)
14 Emmitt Smith (1969)
17 Gary Paulsen (1939)
20 Mary Pope Osborne
 (1949)
22 Arnold Lobel (1933)

June

 5 Richard Scarry (1919)
 6 Cynthia Rylant (1954)
 7 Larisa Oleynik (1981)
10 Maurice Sendak (1928)
 Tara Lipinski (1982)
11 Joe Montana (1956)
13 Tim Allen (1953)
15 Jack Horner (1946)
18 Chris Van Allsburg
 (1949)
25 Eric Carle (1929)

26 Derek Jeter (1974)
 Michael Vick (1980)
30 Robert Ballard (1971)

July

 2 Dave Thomas (1932)
 6 George W. Bush (1946)
 7 Michelle Kwan (1980)
11 E.B. White (1899)
 Patricia Polacco (1944)
12 Kristi Yamaguchi
 (1972)
14 Peggy Parish (1927)
 Laura Numeroff (1953)
18 Nelson Mandela (1918)
24 Barry Bonds (1964)
 Mara Wilson (1987)
26 Jan Berenstain (1923)
28 Beatrix Potter (1866)
 Jim Davis (1945)
31 J.K. Rowling (1965)
 Daniel Radcliffe (1989)

August

 2 Betsy Byars (1928)
 4 Jeff Gordon (1971)
 6 Barbara Cooney (1917)
 David Robinson (1965)
 9 Patricia McKissack
 (1944)
 Whitney Houston
 (1963)
11 Joanna Cole (1944)

August (continued)

12 Walter Dean Myers (1937)
Fredrick McKissack (1939)
Ann M. Martin (1955)
15 Linda Ellerbee (1944)
16 Matt Christopher (1917)
18 Paula Danziger (1944)
19 Bill Clinton (1946)
23 Kobe Bryant (1978)
24 Cal Ripken Jr. (1960)
26 Mother Teresa (1910)
27 Alexandra Nechita (1985)
30 Virginia Lee Burton (1909)
Sylvia Earle (1935)
Donald Crews (1938)
31 Itzhak Perlman (1945)

September

1 Gloria Estefan (1958)
3 Aliki (1929)
7 Briana Scurry (1971)
8 Jack Prelutsky (1940)
Jon Scieszka (1954)
Jonathan Taylor Thomas (1982)
15 Robert McCloskey (1914)
Tomie dePaola (1934)

16 Roald Dahl (1916)
18 Ben Carson (1951)
Lance Armstrong (1971)
24 Jim Henson (1936)
25 Will Smith (1968)
26 Serena Williams (1981)
28 Hilary Duff (1987)
29 Stan Berenstain (1923)
30 Dominique Moceanu (1981)

October

1 Mark McGwire (1963)
5 Grant Hill (1972)
Maya Lin (1959)
6 Lonnie Johnson (1949)
7 Yo-Yo Ma (1955)
8 Faith Ringgold (1930)
9 Zachery Ty Bryan (1981)
10 James Marshall (1942)
12 Marion Jones (1975)
13 Nancy Kerrigan (1969)
17 Mae Jemison (1954)
Nick Cannon (1980)
18 Wynton Marsalis (1961)
22 Ichiro Suzuki (1973)
23 Pele (1940)
25 Pedro Martinez (1971)
26 Hillary Clinton (1947)
Steven Kellogg (1941)

November

3 Janell Cannon (1957)

4 Laura Bush (1946)

9 Lois Ehlert (1934)

12 Sammy Sosa (1968)

14 Astrid Lindgren (1907)
William Steig (1907)
Condoleezza Rice
(1954)

15 Daniel Pinkwater
(1941)

19 Kerri Strug (1977)

21 Ken Griffey Jr. (1969)

25 Marc Brown (1946)

26 Charles Schulz (1922)

27 Bill Nye (1955)
Kevin Henkes (1960)
Jaleel White (1977)

December

1 Jan Brett (1949)

5 Frankie Muniz (1985)

18 Christina Aguilera
(1980)

19 Eve Bunting (1928)

22 Jerry Pinkney (1939)

23 Avi (1937)

26 Susan Butcher (1954)

30 Mercer Mayer (1943)
Tiger Woods (1975)